DK READERS

Level 1

Animal Hide and Seek
Animals at Home
A Bed for the Winter
Big Machines
Born to be a Butterfly
Bugs and Us
Busy Buzzy Bee
A Day at Greenhill Farm
A Day in the Life of a Builder
A Day in the Life of a Firefighter
A Day in the Life of a Teacher
Dinosaur's Day
Diving Dolphin
Duckling Days
Feeding Time
First Day at Gymnastics
Homes Around the World
I Want to Be a Ballerina
Let's Play Soccer
Rockets and Spaceships
Submarines and Submersibles
Surprise Puppy!
Tale of a Tadpole

Train Travel
A Trip to the Dentist
A Trip to the Zoo
Truck Trouble
Whatever the Weather
Wild Baby Animals
Angry Birds Star Wars: Yoda Bird's Heroes
Indiana Jones: Indy's Adventures
John Deere: Good Morning, Farm!
LEGO® DC Super Heroes: Ready for Action!
LEGO® DUPLO: Around Town
LEGO® Pirates: Brickbeard's Treasure
Star Wars The Clone Wars: Ahsoka
  in Action
Star Wars The Clone Wars: Pirates . . .
  and Worse!
Star Wars The Clone Wars: Watch Out for
  Jabba the Hutt!
Star Wars: Luke Skywalker's Amazing Story
Star Wars: Ready, Set, Podrace!
Star Wars: Tatooine Adventures
Star Wars: What is a Wookiee?
Star Wars: Who Saved the Galaxy?

Level 2

Amazing Buildings
Animal Hospital
Astronaut: Living in Space
Boys' Life: Dinosaur Battles
Boys' Life: Tracking
Bugs! Bugs! Bugs!
Dinosaur Dinners
Earth Smart: How to Take Care
  of the Environment
Emperor Penguins
Eruption! The Story of Volcanoes
Fire Fighter!
The Great Migration
Horse Show
I Want to Be a Gymnast
Journey of a Humpback Whale
Let's Go Riding
The Little Ballerina
The Secret Life of Trees
Slinky, Scaly Snakes!
Sniffles, Sneezes, Hiccups, and Coughs
Starry Sky
The Story of Columbus
The Story of Pocahontas
Survivors: The Night the Titanic Sank
Twisters!
Water Everywhere

Winking, Blinking, Wiggling, and Waggling
Angry Birds Star Wars: Lard Vader's Villains
Indiana Jones: Traps and Snares
LEGO® DC Super Heroes: Super-Villains
LEGO® Friends: Let's Go Riding
LEGO® Hero Factory: Brain Attack
LEGO® Hero Factory: Meet the Heroes
LEGO® Kingdoms: Defend the Castle
LEGO® Legends of Chima: Tribes of Chima
LEGO® Monster Fighters: Meet the Monsters
LEGO® Star Wars: Attack of the Clones
LEGO® Star Wars: The Phantom Menace
Pokémon: Meet Ash's Pikachu!
Pokémon: Watch Out for Team Galactic!
Star Wars The Clone Wars: Boba Fett,
  Jedi Hunter
Star Wars The Clone Wars: Chewbacca and
  the Wookiee Warriors
Star Wars: A Queen's Diary
Star Wars: Bounty Hunters for Hire
Star Wars: Join the Rebels
Star Wars: The Adventures of Han Solo
WWE: CM Punk
WWE: Hornswoggle
WWE: John Cena
WWE: Rey Mysterio
X-Men: Meet the X-Men

A Note to Parents

DK READERS is a compelling program for beginning readers, designed in conjunction with leading literacy experts, including Dr. Linda Gambrell, Distinguished Professor of Education at Clemson University. Dr. Gambrell has served as President of the National Reading Conference, the College Reading Association, and the International Reading Association.

Beautiful illustrations and superb full-color photographs combine with engaging, easy-to-read stories to offer a fresh approach to each subject in the series. Each DK READER is guaranteed to capture a child's interest while developing his or her reading skills, general knowledge, and love of reading.

The five levels of DK READERS are aimed at different reading abilities, enabling you to choose the books that are exactly right for your child:

Pre-level 1: Learning to read
Level 1: Beginning to read
Level 2: Beginning to read alone
Level 3: Reading alone
Level 4: Proficient readers

The "normal" age at which a child begins to read can be anywhere from three to eight years old. Adult participation through the lower levels is very helpful for providing encouragement, discussing storylines, and sounding out unfamiliar words.

No matter which level you select, you can be sure that you are helping your child learn to read, then read to learn!

LONDON, NEW YORK, MUNICH,
MELBOURNE, AND DELHI

Editor Lisa Stock
Art Editor Toby Truphet
Managing Editor Laura Gilbert
Design Manager Maxine Pedliham
Publishing Manager Julie Ferris
Publishing Director Simon Beecroft
Pre-Production Producer Marc Staples
Reading Consultant Dr. Linda Gambrell

DK India
Editor Rahul Ganguly
Senior Editor Garima Sharma
Assistant Art Editors Karan Chaudhary,
Chitrak Srivastava
Deputy Managing Art Editor Neha Ahuja
Pre-Production Manager Sunil Sharma
DTP Designer Manish Upreti

For Lucasfilm
Executive Editor J.W. Rinzler
Art Director Troy Alders
Keeper of the Holocron Leland Chee
Director of Publishing Carol Roeder

First American Edition, 2013
13 14 15 16 10 9 8 7 6 5 4 3 2 1
001-195156-Nov/13
Published in the United States by DK Publishing
345 Hudson Street, New York, New York 10014

Published in Great Britain by Dorling Kindersley Limited

A catalog record for this book is available
from the Library of Congress.

ISBN: 978-1-4654-1415-1 (Paperback)
ISBN: 978-1-4654-1416-8 (Hardcover)

Color reproduction by Altaimage, UK
Printed and bound by L-Rex Printing Co., Ltd, China

Discover more at
www.dk.com
www.starwars.com

Contents

DK READERS

BEGINNING
1
TO READ

STAR WARS

ARE EWOKS SCARED OF STORMTROOPERS?

Written by Catherine Saunders

Unlikely heroes

Being big and strong does not mean you will win every battle.

Heroes can come in all shapes and sizes.

Wicket

Anakin Skywalker

Jar Jar Binks

Sometimes it is the ones you least expect who save the day.

As Master Yoda wisely says, "Size matters not."

R2-D2

Master Yoda

Furry warriors

These stormtroopers are following evil orders on the forest moon of Endor.

The small, furry Ewoks who live there have no armor or blasters … but they aren't scared of the stormtroopers!

The brave Ewoks fight with stones and spears to save their forest home.

Daring rebel

The Death Star is a huge weapon with the power to destroy a whole planet.

Can young rebel pilot Luke Skywalker defeat a weapon the size of a small moon?

Yes! He flies his X-wing right up to the Death Star and destroys it with a well-aimed blast!

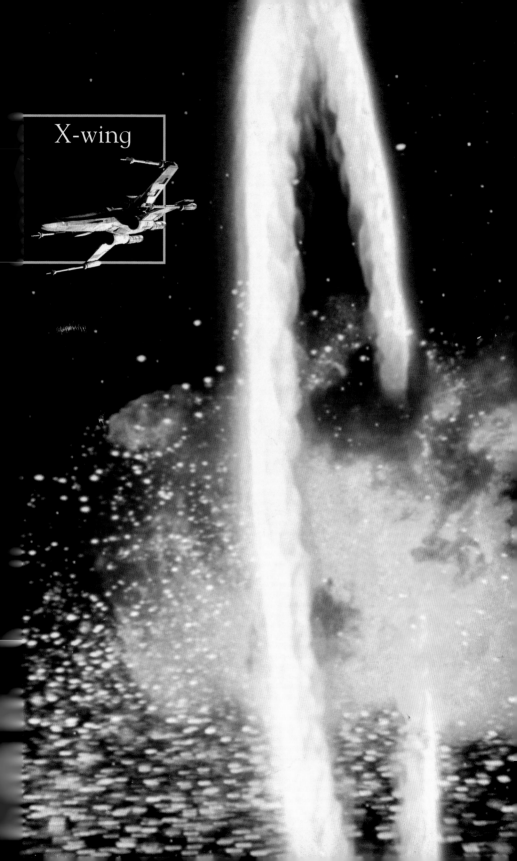

X-wing

Battling Binks

Watch out! These battle droids are armed.

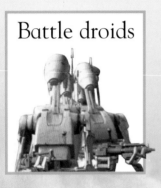
Battle droids

Sometimes a clumsy general can actually be a help in battle!

Jar Jar Binks

Energy ball

Jar Jar Binks accidentally releases some energy balls.

Smash! A whole group of battle droids is wiped out.

Droid
Control Ship

Child's play

Anakin Skywalker is only
nine years old, but he is a very
brave pilot.

Anakin

Starfighter

In a space battle, little Anakin flies his starfighter inside the Droid Control Ship undetected.

He hits just the spot to destroy the ship and win the battle!

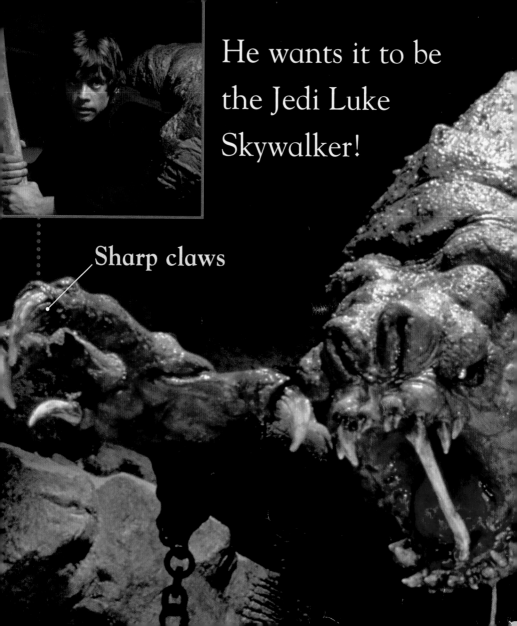

He wants it to be the Jedi Luke Skywalker!

Sharp claws

The rancor may be bigger,
but Luke is much smarter.

Luke traps the scary beast
and escapes to safety.

Princess in peril

Jabba the Hutt is a crime lord.
He takes Princess Leia prisoner
as his slave.

It looks like she
will never escape!

**Princess
Leia**

The princess patiently waits until Jabba is distracted.

Then Leia uses her chains to defeat the huge Hutt.

Jabba

Working together

Jedi Obi-Wan Kenobi is about to be eaten by a fierce acklay.

Obi-Wan cannot escape his wild opponent alone.

Jedi

Obi-Wan Kenobi

Luckily, he isn't alone for long!

Obi-Wan's friends arrive riding on a reek, just in time to carry him away.

Reek

Acklay

AT-AT attack

The AT-ATs are huge walking tanks on legs.

The rebel pilots cannot defeat them by firepower alone.

Snowspeeder

Luckily, the rebels have a brilliant plan.

They trip up the AT-ATs using cables fired from their snowspeeders.

21

Nimble Jedi

The Sith Lords Darth Sidious and Dooku are very powerful.

Jedi Master Yoda is very powerful, too, but he is also very small.

Darth
Sidious

Master
Yoda

Despite his size, the Jedi jumps and leaps extremely fast.

Even the Sith Lords cannot defeat him in a duel.

Dooku

Smart thinking

A Star Destroyer is chasing a rebel ship called the *Millennium Falcon.*

Rebel pilot Han Solo tries to lose the huge Star Destroyer by leading it into an asteroid field.

Han Solo

Han knows that his small ship can dart between the space rocks, but the Star Destroyer is much too big to do that!

Millennium Falcon

Star Destroyer

Droid vs. droid

A little droid like
R2-D2 doesn't
scare these big, bad
super battle droids.

R2-D2

But they should
be scared!

Tiny R2-D2 squirts
the super battle
droids with oil and
then sets them on fire.

Super battle droid

Brave leader

A new, even bigger Death Star has been built!

Han Solo's friend Lando Calrissian is leading a dangerous mission to attack it.

He flies the *Millennium Falcon* inside the Death Star and helps his team to destroy it.

The galaxy is free!

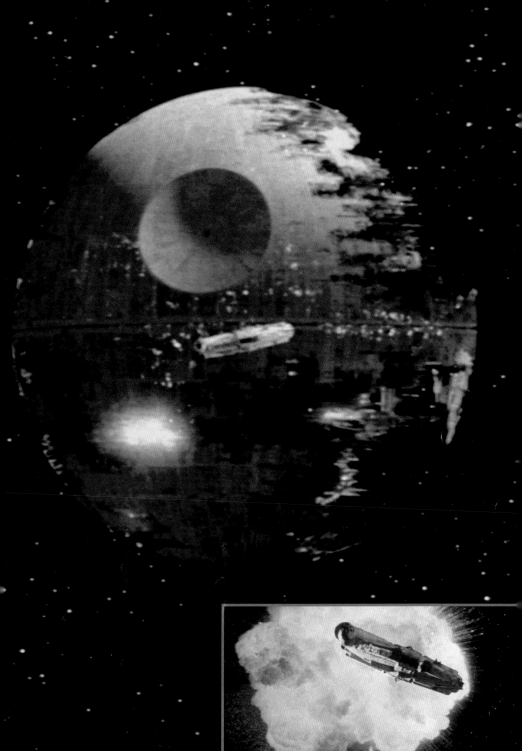

Victory!

Now you have met some of the galaxy's greatest and least likely heroes.

They may be younger, weaker, or smaller than their enemies, but they have great courage.

Would you be as brave as them?

Glossary

Battle droids
Soldier droids made for fighting.

Jedi
A member of a group that fights evil.

Snowspeeder
A flying vehicle that can travel over snow.

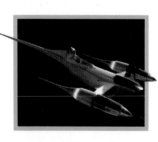

Starfighter
A small spacecraft that can take sharp turns.

X-wing
A one-man spacecraft with excellent weapons.

Index

 READERS

My name is

_____

I have read this book ☑

Date

_____